Books should be returned or renewed by the
last date stamped above

J 780·9

CHARTER MARK

Awarded for excellence
to Arts & Libraries

Kent
County
Council

20TH CENTURY MUSIC

80s & 90s

DIFFERENT PATHS

20TH CENTURY MUSIC – '80s & '90s
was produced by

David West 👬 **Children's Books**
7 Princeton Court
55 Felsham Road
London SW15 1AZ

Picture Research: Carrie Haines
Designer: Rob Shone
Editor: James Pickering

First published in Great Britain in 2001 by
Heinemann Library, Halley Court, Jordan Hill,
Oxford OX2 8EJ, a division of Reed Educational and
Professional Publishing Limited.

OXFORD MELBOURNE AUCKLAND
JOHANNESBURG BLANTYRE GABORONE
IBADAN PORTSMOUTH (NH) USA CHICAGO

05 04 03 02 01
10 9 8 7 6 5 4 3 2 1

ISBN 0 431 14215 7 (HB)
ISBN 0 431 14222 X (PB)

British Library Cataloguing in Publication Data

Hayes, Malcolm
The 80s & 90s: different paths. - (20th century
music)
1. Music - 20th century - Juvenile literature
I. Title II. Nineteen hundred and eighty - two
thousand
780.9'04

Printed and bound in Italy

PHOTO CREDITS :
Abbreviations: t-top, m-middle, b-bottom, r-right,
l-left.

Front cover m - (AA/DR 9019) Redferns, br -
(Malcolm Crowther) Redferns. 12br, 14tm, 17tl, 22-
23t, 23m & b (David Redfern), 5br, 14bl, 17m, 19m
& b, 20b (Ebet Roberts), 4t & 22l, 19tr (Mick
Hutson), 15ml, 17tr (Bob King), 3 & 15tl (Paul
Bergen), 20-21t (Tim Hall), 18l (Richie Aaron), 27tr
(Malcolm Crowther), 15br (Sue Cunningham), 16br
(Kieran Doherty), 22b (J. Krebbs), 22m (Chi Modu),
21tr (Albert Ortega), 5tr (Roberta Parkin), 24l (Nicky
J. Simms), 16tr (Peter Still), 20t (Jon Super) - Redferns.
4b & 26bl, 6l, 6-7t, 7m, 8br, 9bl, 11r, 25tr, 26t - Betty
Freeman/Lebrecht Collection. 6r, 8-9t - Alastair
Muir/Lebrecht Collection. 24r, 28bl - Nigel
Luckhurst/Lebrecht Collection. 25bl, 27m - Richard
H. Smith/Lebrecht Collection. 28r - Alexandra
Kremer/Lebrecht Collection. 10bl - Suzie
Maecler/Lebrecht Collection. 13t - Laurie
Lewis/Lebrecht Collection. 29tr - David
Farrell/Lebrecht Collection. 29m - Victor
Bazlenov/Lebrecht Collection. 29bl - Sally
Whyte/Lebrecht Collection. 26br - Lebrecht
Collection. 27b - Brooker/Rex Features. 18tr - Rex
Features. 5tl - Frank Forcino/LFI-UFF/London
Features Int. Ltd. 16bl - Flpo Musto/LFI-IM/London
Features Int. Ltd. 10mr - Sally Chappell/The Art
Archive/Victoria and Albert Museum. 12tr - The
Kobal Collection. 8l - Mark Taylor. 9mr - Robert
Lowell/Hulton Getty. 13m & b - Performing Art
Library.

Front cover: Madonna (main image), John Tavener.

*The dates in brackets after a person's name
give the years that he or she lived.*

*An explanation of difficult words can be
found in the glossary on page 30.*

20TH CENTURY MUSIC

80s & 90s
DIFFERENT PATHS

Malcolm Hayes

Heinemann
LIBRARY

CONTENTS

STILL THE MASTER
Illness had taken its toll on Miles Davis (1926–91), but in the early 1980s he re-established himself as one of jazz's greatest ever trumpeters.

RISING STAR
George Benjamin (born 1960) studied with Messiaen in Paris, and quickly made his name with his orchestral work Ringed by the Flat Horizon (1980).

A COMFORTABLE AGE – PERHAPS TOO COMFORTABLE?

*NIRVANA
Kurt Cobain (1967–94) led Nirvana to huge success with the albums* Nevermind *(1991) and In Utero (1993).*

5

The closing decades of the 20th century were a time of strange contradictions. By the mid-1990s the Communist governments of the east European states and Russia had fallen, to be replaced by often troubled experiments in western-style democracy. In the West there followed an age of apparent political stability and economic prosperity. The times were therefore steadier. They were also duller. Compared with the liberated 1960s and the revolution-pursuing 1970s, the musical waves of the 20th century's last two decades rolled less high than before. Instead, this was more the era of the creative individualist.

In classical music, rock and jazz, styles and techniques – and the possibility of mixing them – were more varied than ever. Music seemed to be everywhere, especially with the huge growth of specialist radio stations and the arrival of the compact disc. But different musical styles became pigeonholed and more separate than before – when they tried to blend with each other, confusion and blandness were often the result. Truly strong individual talents, meanwhile, grew and flourished as they always have.

MINIMALISM: ADAMS AND OPERA

Minimalism, with its emphasis on conventional, listener-friendly harmony and easy-to-follow musical 'pattern-making', appealed as strongly to the new age of musical 'accessibility' as modernism did not. But its best composers achieved works that soared far above predictable mediocrity.

MUSICAL LANDSCAPES
John Adams, at Tilden Park near Berkeley, California. The long harmonic reach of his music is rooted in the European symphonic tradition of the 19th and early 20th centuries, especially Sibelius.

A REMARKABLE FIRST OPERA

America's John Adams (born 1947) made his international breakthrough with *Harmonium* (1980), for chorus and orchestra. The music's sonic appeal, range of invention and sheer drama all indicated the arrival of a composer with major potential. Adams followed this up with the first of his operas, *Nixon in China*, first staged at the Houston Opera in 1987. This showed that a minimalist-based technique could also have the inventive range to make a large-scale opera work impressively on the stage, both in musical and in dramatic terms.

Nixon (at foot of steps) arrives in China, in Adams's opera.

REALISTIC OPERA

Adams's *Nixon in China* portrayed the events of Richard Nixon's visit – the first by an American president – to the Communist People's Republic of China in 1972. It brilliantly combined a documentary approach – 'opera as reporting', almost – with a musical imagination and dramatic effectiveness that connected clearly with operatic tradition.

6

7

WORKING TOGETHER

Steve Reich (centre, rear) rehearsing with his ensemble. The interplay between Reich's favourite line-up of percussion instruments is much harder to perform than it sounds: each concert needs intensive preparation.

POLITICAL CONFLICT

Adams's next opera, *The Death of Klinghoffer* (1991), was fiercely controversial. It portrayed the hijacking of the cruise ship *Achille Lauro* in the Mediterranean Sea by a group of armed Palestinians, the shooting of an elderly Jewish passenger, and also the wider political troubles of the Middle East that lay behind these events. Adams's latest large-scale work is *El Niño* (2000), an oratorio about the Christmas nativity story, using Spanish and Latin besides English texts.

COMPOSING FOR THE THEATRE

The oddly-spelt the CIVIL warS *was a huge project devised by theatre director Robert Wilson, involving several composers: Glass (above) completed Act V – 'The Rome Section' in 1983. The Representative from Planet 8 (1987) was based on Doris Lessing's science-fiction story.*

JOURNEY TO ANCIENT EGYPT

In Akhnaten, *Glass suggested the story's distant time and place by creating a deliberately strange sound: there are no violins, so that the orchestral colouring is much darker than usual.*

GLASS AND REICH

Steve Reich (born 1936) produced large-scale works in *Tehillim* (1981) and *The Desert Music* (1983) for chorus and orchestra. Philip Glass (born 1937) achieved wide success with two operas: *Satyagraha* (staged in 1980), about the non-violent resistance movement created by Mahatma Gandhi, and *Akhnaten* (1984), about an Ancient Egyptian pharaoh. Glass also composed a film score, *Koyaanisqatsi* (1982).

MODERNISM: BIRTWISTLE AND CARTER

As audiences for classical music grew and became wealthier, they mostly wanted – or believed they wanted – music that seemed easier to listen to. But modernism was far from dead, as its leading composers magnificently showed.

BIRTWISTLE'S ROOTS

Birtwistle is now a world-famous composer, but he remains in touch with his roots in Lancashire. In *The Mask of Orpheus*, the hero crosses to the Underworld and back again across a bridge with 17 arches – like the railway viaduct by the town of Accrington, where Birtwistle was born.

Accrington Viaduct inspired one of the great scenes of modern opera.

ORPHEUS SINGS ON AN EPIC SCALE

English composer Harrison Birtwistle (born 1934) worked on his massive three-act opera, *The Mask of Orpheus*, for ten years before completing it in 1983. It is about the singer of Ancient Greek legend, who visited the underworld to try to bring his dead bride, Euridice, back to life. Birtwistle's score presents the story in a ritualistic, multi-layered way, so that in places, different versions of the Orpheus legend are presented on stage at the same time. The result is a musical drama of immense power.

MUSICAL INDIVIDUALISTS
Birtwistle (right) with Alfred Brendel (born 1931), the Austrian-born pianist who plays mostly classical works, and who is also deeply interested in modern music.

BIRTWISTLE: MORE OPERAS

Birtwistle's next opera was *Gawain* (1991). This takes a similar, multi-layered approach to the story of Sir Gawain, one of the knights of King Arthur's Round Table in Celtic legend, and tells of Gawain's duel with Arthur's enemy, the sinister Green Knight. Birtwistle's most recent opera is *The Last Supper* (2000), about the Biblical story of Jesus and his disciples, viewed from the perspective of the turbulent and war-torn 20th century.

CARTER: EVER THE EXPLORER

Some composers mellow with age. America's Elliott Carter (born 1908), on the contrary, came up with works full of even busier and more complex invention than before, such as his large-scale, three-movement *Symphonia* (1993–96). His song-cycle *In Sleep, in Thunder* (1981) set words by the American poet, Robert Lowell. At the age of 90, Carter completed his first opera, *What Next?*. It was first staged in Berlin in 1999.

THE GREEN KNIGHT SINGS
When Gawain decapitates the Green Knight in a duel, the severed head goes on singing.

ROBERT LOWELL
An important American poet of the 20th century, he and his words had also inspired Benjamin Britten's cantata Phaedra.

CARTER AND KNUSSEN
The success of Carter's later music has owed much to the conducting expertise of Oliver Knussen (right, born 1952), whose own works include two operas, Where the Wild Things Are *(1983) and* Higglety Pigglety Pop! *(1985).*

FRANCE: MESSIAEN AND BOULEZ

Classical music in France, too, was dominated by two greatly influential, and very different master-composers. The musical history of the second half of the 20th century would have been different without them.

THE SAINT AND THE WINGED SINGERS

Olivier Messiaen (1908–92) worked on his only opera, *Saint François d'Assise*, between 1975 and 1983, when it was first staged at the Paris Opera. It tells the story of the life and death of the medieval Italian saint, Francis of Assisi, in a sequence of eight, fresco-like scenes. Some of these are very large. St Francis's sermon to the birds lasts over an hour, and is the grandest and most elaborate example of Messiaen's technique of transcribing birdsong in musical terms.

FREQUENT VISITOR TO ENGLAND
Messiaen with the conductor John Carewe. In the Eighties, Messiaen's music was performed more in England than in France.

SACRED SPIRIT

For Messiaen, music was a manifestation of God's presence on Earth. He described his lifelong Catholic faith as 'the one aspect of my life that I will not regret at the hour of my death'. Until age prevented him, he continued to play the organ at Mass every Sunday in the Church of Sainte-Trinité in Paris, as he had since the 1930s.

The Transfiguration *by the English artist William Blake (1757–1827), who, like Messiaen, was inspired by religious themes.*

MESSIAEN'S LAST THOUGHTS

Messiaen's interest in birdsong was both musical and symbolic. For him, each bird represented a soul resurrected from the dead by Christ's self-sacrifice, and its song expressed that soul's eternal joy. Birdsong also features in Messiaen's largest organ work, *Livre du Saint Sacrement* (Book of the Holy Sacrament, 1984–86). His last major creation was *Eclairs sur l'au-delà* (Rays on the Beyond, 1989–92), in ten orchestral movements.

MICROCHIP MUSIC
What used to be bulky equipment has become easily portable. Today, a computer able to generate or transform sounds in a live performance can be set up in venues ranging in size from a concert hall to a home studio.

COMPOSING WITH COMPUTERS

Pierre Boulez (born 1925) divided his time between his worldwide conducting career and his work as director of IRCAM (Institut de Recherche et Coordination Acoustique/Musique), the centre in Paris for research into computer-generated musical sound. Boulez has produced two ongoing 'works in progress' involving conventional instruments and computers: *Explosante-fixe* (Exploding-stationary, originally begun in 1971) and *Répons* (Response(s), begun in 1981). He also re-composed his early cantata *Le Visage Nuptial* (The Nuptial Countenance, 1946) for soloists, chorus and large orchestra, completing this in 1989.

STILL PIONEERING
Boulez is still committed to exploring the musical possibilities opened up by the use of computer-manipulated sound.

NATURE'S MUSIC
Messiaen could transcribe even the fastest and highest-pitched birdsong by slowing it down, lowering it, and also by harmonizing it.

Musicals

The stage musical had long been an American speciality. But it was England that now produced one of the most successful composers of musicals ever, whose work swept the world.

MEGASTAR OF THE MUSICAL STAGE

Andrew Lloyd Webber (born 1948) is the son of the composer William Lloyd Webber (1914–82), and brother of cellist Julian Lloyd Webber (born 1951). His earlier successes in musicals had included *Joseph and the Amazing Technicolour Dreamcoat* (1968, expanded 1972), *Jesus Christ Superstar* (1971) and *Evita* (1978). Now came *Cats* (1981, based on poems by T. S. Eliot), *Starlight Express* (1984), and *The Phantom of the Opera* (1986). Early in 2001, these three were all still running at London theatres.

A VERSATILE GIFT

Lloyd Webber's talent is in being able to work in different styles suitable to each project, while keeping his own unmistakable musical signature. *Cats* mixes song, spoken dialogue and dance in the classic manner; *Starlight Express* is closer to a rock musical; and *The Phantom of the Opera* has long 'through-composed' passages like opera. Other Lloyd Webber hits are *Aspects of Love* (1989) and *Sunset Boulevard* (1993).

LATIN AMERICAN HEROINE

Lloyd Webber's most famous lyricist is Tim Rice, although *Evita* turned out to be their final collaboration. It was based on the life of Evita Duarte, wife of the populist Argentinian president Juan Perón. In 1996 Warner Brothers released a film version with Madonna (p. 18) in the title role. For this, Rice and Lloyd Webber wrote an additional song, 'You Must Love Me'.

Madonna in the role of Evita

HIS OWN MAN

A rare picture of the limelight-avoiding Andrew Lloyd Webber performing. His newest musical, with lyrics by Ben Elton, is The Beautiful Game (2000), about football-loving teenagers in the Sixties.

12

A BROADWAY ORIGINAL

Both lyricist and composer, Stephen Sondheim is the undisputed king of the modern Broadway musical.

SONDHEIM: AN AMERICAN MASTER

Stephen Sondheim (born 1930) came to fame as the brilliant lyricist of Leonard Bernstein's *West Side Story* in 1957. His own musicals often explore unusual subjects in innovative ways. *Sunday in the Park with George* (1984) is set in Paris, and was inspired by a painting by Georges Seurat which hangs in the Art Institute of Chicago. *Into the Woods* (1991) is based on the Grimm Brothers' fairy tales, while *Passion* (1994) is set in 1860s Italy.

REVOLUTION ON STAGE

Based on Victor Hugo's novel of revolutionary France, Cameron Mackintosh's production of Alain Boublil's and Claude-Michel Schönberg's Les Misérables opened in London in 1985. It's still running.

MODERN FABLE

In Sondheim's Into the Woods, familiar fairy-tale characters – Red Riding Hood, Jack the Giant-Killer and Cinderella – encounter nightmare situations unfamiliar from their stories, before optimism and happiness are restored at the end.

EMBRACING THE WORLD: GRACELAND

After the glutted excesses of the 1970s, rock needed to explore new musical territory. Much as people in the increasingly affluent 1980s were travelling more widely than ever before, music began to do the same.

MUSICAL ROOTS
Hugh Masekela was a co-founder of the Jazz Epistles, the first black South African band to record a jazz album.

14

SIMON STIRS UP CONTROVERSY
Paul Simon (centre, in white shirt) performing Graceland *with Ladysmith Black Mambazo. He was accused of exploiting black musicians for his own ends, but* Graceland *did much to increase the global success of world music.*

PAUL SIMON MAKES NEW FRIENDS

After his successes in his duo with Art Garfunkel (born 1941), Paul Simon (born 1941) found a new direction in *Graceland* (1986). This started from tapes he made of South African musicians, which he then worked on further in New York. The result was 'world music' that brought unfamiliar aspects of black African music to white, western ears. Simon followed this with *The Rhythm of the Saints* (1990), which features Brazilian drumming.

LATE, BUT SWEET SUCCESS

In 1996, five elderly Cuban folk and jazz musicians were brought together to record a one-off album, *Buena Vista Social Club*. It caught the world-music mood of the 1990s and achieved a legendary success for the group known locally as *los superabuelos* ('the super-grandfathers'). German film-maker Wim Wenders made a documentary of their sell-out concerts in Amsterdam and at New York's Carnegie Hall in 1998.

Cuban old-timers with guitarist Ry Cooder (right)

OUT OF AFRICA

Among those appearing on *Graceland* were the Zulu group Ladysmith Black Mambazo. They went on to world fame with albums including *Shaka Zulu* (produced by Paul Simon, 1987) and *The Star and the Wise Man* (with Simon and country singer Dolly Parton, 1998). South Africa's trumpet- and flugelhorn-player Hugh Masekela (born 1939) developed a style of Afro-American jazz that had a huge following both at home and in America.

GOING SOLO

David Byrne (born 1952) took a break from his group Talking Heads in 1980, and collaborated with Brian Eno (born 1948) in *My Life in the Bush of Ghosts*. This featured Egyptian singers and Islamic chant, while in *Rei Momo* (1989) Byrne is backed by Brazilian musicians. Sting (Gordon Sumner, born 1951), formerly of the group the Police, made his first solo album, the jazz-rock crossover *Dream of the Blue Turtles,* in 1985. He also became involved in the ecological threat to the Brazilian Indian population with his Rainforest Foundation.

STING GOES NATIVE
For a time Sting was more involved in his ecological work than with music. In 1989, he took the Indian Chief Raoni on a worldwide publicity tour.

GOING HIS OWN WAY
In 1989, David Byrne (pictured here on a visit to Moscow) left Talking Heads and concentrated on albums more influenced by world music, including Uh-Oh *(1992) and* Feelings *(1997).*

ROCK: THE BANDS

On both sides of the Atlantic, spectacularly successful bands drew their fans to their huge stadium concerts. But the one with as much pulling-power as any of them had also been around the longest.

Geldof (left) with U2's lead singer Bono at Live Aid

THE STONES KEEP ON ROLLING

Since their heady rock 'n' roll successes of the Sixties, the Rolling Stones had never lost their star appeal, especially in America. In 1981, they broke new ground by planning and organizing the first tour which took 1970s-style stadium rock around the world, complete with new songs, massive amplification, and exotic and spectacular light shows. After *Tattoo You* (1981) came other tours and albums every few years, including *Bridges to Babylon* (1997), with vocalist Mick Jagger and guitarist Keith Richards still leading the show.

BROTHERS (UP) IN ARMS
Oasis brothers Liam (left) and Noel Gallagher are notorious for quarrelling bitterly with each other. This tension is not always good for the band, and has led to walkouts.

TIMELESS APPEAL
Middle-aged rock groups with middle-aged fans are no longer rare, and the Stones have expertly survived and prospered through every change of musical fashion.

HELPING THE HUNGRY

The Live Aid concert in 1985, at London's Wembley Stadium and JFK Stadium, Philadelphia, was the idea of Bob Geldof (born 1954) of the Boomtown Rats. He organized the show to raise money for the victims of African famine. Many of rock's leading artists agreed to appear for free, including U2, Queen and Mick Jagger. Supergroups Led Zeppelin and the Who reformed specially for the event.

MUSICIANSHIP
Led by Michael Stipe (right), R.E.M. countered the excesses of stadium rock with their exceptional songwriting skills.

BRITPOP: OASIS

The vast success of Oasis showed that rock was in the mood for something along the lines of Sixties pop, recycled with a sharp 1990s edge. Formed in Manchester in 1993 by the Gallagher brothers, Liam (vocals) and talented songwriter Noel (guitar), the group's albums *Definitely Maybe* (1994) and *(What's the Story) Morning Glory?* (1995) hurtled the group to world fame. Radiohead, formed at an Oxford public school in 1988, offered an angrier contrast with *Pablo Honey* (1993), *The Bends* (1995) and *OK Computer* (1997).

BREAKING ALL RECORDS
Live Aid was the world's biggest ever television event. Geldof came on stage to ask the watching billions for donations.

WE WILL ROCK YOU
Live Aid inspired the Queen song 'One Vision'. More hits followed, until singer Freddie Mercury's death in 1991.

SHORT NAMES, BIG AIMS: U2, R.E.M.

Ireland's U2 and their lead singer Bono (Paul Hewson, born 1960) had already made their name with their ambitious and politically controversial albums *War* (1983) and *The Unforgettable Fire* (1984), when their session at Live Aid dazzled the world. America's pacesetters were R.E.M., encompassing raging electric tracks and gentle acoustic ones in *Out of Time* (1991), *Automatic for the People* (1992) and *Up* (1998).

ROCK: THE SONGWRITERS

Rock's range of singer-songwriters was as varied as ever. Record companies and radio stations increasingly pitched performers' work at particular groups of listeners, in a way that was far from the 'Graceland' spirit (pp. 14–15) of different musical worlds coming together.

One of the last pictures of Lennon, in his New York apartment

TWO DIFFERENT WOMEN

The most successful female rock artist ever, Madonna (Madonna Ciccone, born 1958) hit stardom with *Like a Virgin* (1984). Her later albums included *Like a Prayer* (1989) and *Something to Remember* (1995), showing both her songwriting talent and her flair for re-inventing her image. Less prolific, and with a passionate following in Britain, Kate Bush (born 1958) recorded the adventurous *Hounds of Love* (1985), *The Sensual World* (1989), and *The Red Shoes* (1993).

MULTIPLE ROLES
Madonna's success as a singer has been matched by her film appearances in Desperately Seeking Susan *(1984) – which featured one of her best songs, 'Into the Groove' – and* Evita *(p. 12).*

A LIFE CUT SHORT

The up-and-down post-Beatles career of John Lennon (1940–80) had included some fine material on *John Lennon and the Plastic Ono Band* (1971) and *Imagine* (1971). In late 1980, Lennon emerged after five years' retirement to record *Double Fantasy*, and was working on another album, *Milk and Honey*, when he was shot dead by an obsessed fan in the street outside his New York home.

THREE MEGASTARS

After making his album *Listen Without Prejudice, Vol. 1* (1990), George Michael (Giorgios Panayiotou, born 1963) sued his record company, Sony, for 'seeing artists as little more than software'. He lost, but a compromise settlement was worked out. Michael later recorded his successful *Older* (1996). Prince (Prince Rogers Nelson, born 1958) quickly emerged as a major and intelligent musical talent; one of his hugest successes was *Purple Rain* (1984). Michael Jackson (born 1958), one of the original Jackson Five brothers, became the soloist whose *Thriller* (1982) has sold 40 million copies, which was a world record for nearly 20 years.

AMERICAN ROOTS

Garth Brooks (born 1962) is the successful king of country and western music, whose vast commercial appeal contrasts with the more folk-rooted, newly revived world of bluegrass fiddle music. And Bruce Springsteen (born 1949) achieved immortality with his storming live performances and his portrayal of the dark side of the American Dream on the album *Born in the USA* (1984).

In 1993 Prince announced that he would be renamed as an icon (as above). Most fans preferred TAFKAP – The Artist Formerly Known As Prince.

COUNTRY MEGASTAR
Despite country music's limited appeal outside America, Garth Brooks is probably the world's biggest selling recording artist today.

HIGH-TECH PIONEER
Michael Jackson made elaborate videos to help promote his recordings. The Thriller video's choreography and special effects set new standards for the medium.

HOUSE, HIP-HOP AND RAP

Unlike classical music with its emphasis on melody and harmony, much popular music throughout the 20th century had been about rhythm. House, rap and hip-hop were the late 20th-century essence of music that existed to be danced to.

THE PRODIGY'S KEITH FLINT
The Prodigy is one of the few British bands to top the charts in America in recent years.

THE BEASTIE BOYS
Licensed to Ill (1986) and Check Your Head *(1992) were two of the New York trio's huge-selling albums.*

DANCE TILL YOU DROP

House developed in Chicago, overlapping with the slightly smoother garage and the more rhythmically fixated techno. Steve 'Silk' Hurley came up with house's first No. 1 chart-topper, 'Jack Your Body', in 1987. By the early 1990s, the movement had swept England. The Prodigy starred with their albums *Experience* (1992) and *Music for The Jilted Generation* (1995), and the singles 'Firestarter' and 'Breathe' (both 1996).

HOT SPOT

Manchester's Hacienda Club opened in 1982, and became a huge dance-music attraction in the city now known as 'Madchester'. The non-stop rhythmic bouncing and pounding of bands such as the Happy Mondays and the Stone Roses dominated in the late 1980s. New Order anticipated the rougher mood of 1990s dance music with their single 'Blue Monday' and their album *Power, Corruption and Lies* (both 1983).

New Order evolved from punk band Joy Division.

NICE GUY

Will Smith is the only major rap artist to avoid using bad language. His film appearances have included Independence Day *(1996) and* Men in Black *(1997).*

NO COMPROMISE

Ice-T appears to be proud of a violent past in which he was shot twice during an armed robbery. His albums include Rhyme Pays *(1987) and* Original Gangster *(1991).*

RAP'S ROOTS

Hip-hop began among the black communities of New York. Disc jockeys started switching suddenly between records playing on different turntables, while a colleague improvised high-speed spoken dialogue over the music's changes. This was the art of 'rapping' (a term borrowed from jazz). It soon became an expression of rebellious youth culture, personified by groups such as Public Enemy, Run DMC, and the Beastie Boys. Will Smith (born 1968) conveyed a happier attitude in *He's the DJ, I'm the Rapper* (1988) and *Big Willie Style* (1997).

THE DARK SIDE OF RAP

Gangsta rap had links with the gangland underworld, where violent feuds between artists, managements and record labels became a regular occurrence. Rap superstars Tupac Shakur (1971–96) and Notorious B.I.G (1972–97) were both shot in these circumstances. Prominent survivors included Ice-T (O'Shea Jackson, born 1969), Puff Daddy (Sean 'Puffy' Combs, born 1970) and the band NWA, whose lead vocalist Ice Cube (Tracy Morrow, born 1959) went solo. Public Enemy supported rap's Stop the Violence movement in the late 1980s.

JAZZ: CROSSING OVER

The 'coming together' mood of world music also influenced jazz, which now found ways of absorbing ethnic material alongside the rock element of jazz fusion. Several of jazz's greatest artists were also fine classical performers as well.

ULTIMATE MASTERY

The fantastically gifted Keith Jarrett (born 1945) gave a remarkable series of concerts, often solo, sometimes in a standard jazz trio (with bass and drums), and always on acoustic piano. Many of these have been recorded on the ECM label (p. 28), including legendary solo improvisations in Vienna (1991) and at Milan's La Scala opera house (1995). Jazz's world-music connection reached Jarrett too, in *Spirits* (1985), with its Pakistani flute and ethnic chanting. He also continued playing classical music, making an outstanding recording of Mozart's Piano Concertos (1996).

KEITH JARRETT
Jarrett's reign as the supreme solo jazz pianist was enhanced by the recognition he received for his recordings of three of Mozart's Piano Concertos with the Stuttgart Chamber Orchestra in 1996. The illness Chronic Fatigue Syndrome then forced him to start cancelling concerts.

MILES DAVIS
After several years of ill health, Davis returned to performing in 1980, marking his comeback with the albums We Want Miles *(1981) and* A Night in Tunisia *(1986).*

22

The classically trained Wynton Marsalis (born 1961) played trumpet in the 1984 recording of Leonard Bernstein's *West Side Story*, and also with his own seven-piece band, in *Blue Interlude* (1991). His saxophonist brother, Branford (born 1960), tackled a fusion of jazz and hip-hop (pp. 20–21) in *Buckshot LeFonque* (1994). He also played on Sting's first two solo albums (p. 15), and with Herbie Hancock.

The Marsalis brothers introduced jazz to a new audience in the 1980s.

KINGS OF THE KEYBOARDS

Herbie Hancock (born 1940) was classically trained, but made his name as a highly imaginative jazz-fusion composer and performer, often on electronic keyboards. *Future Shock* (1983) was an admired collaboration with the rock group Rockit, and *Gershwin's World* (1998) was Hancock's unconventional tribute in George Gershwin's centenary year. He also worked and toured with fellow-pianist Chick Corea (born 1941), who in 1994 recorded some Mozart, and the next year composed his own Piano Concerto.

23

HERBIE HANCOCK
Among Hancock's important albums were Quartet *(1981),* Hot and Heavy *(1984) and* A Tribute to Miles *(1992).*

TALENT TWICE OVER

The two Brecker Brothers, trumpeter Randy (born 1945) and saxophonist Michael (born 1949), were already a talented duo. After going solo, they started giving concerts together again, as in *Return of the Brecker Brothers* (1992). Michael pioneered the EWI (Electronic Wind Instrument), a kind of extended saxophone with a huge, nine-octave range. He also toured with Paul Simon (pp. 14–15).

THE BRECKER BROTHERS
Randy Brecker (right) studied classical trumpet at school and then played with Art Blakey and Stevie Wonder among others. Michael played saxophone in the band Steps Ahead before leading his own group.

ITALY AND GERMANY

As in Britain and America, the best of modern classical music in continental Europe was dominated by a few individuals. Their powers of creative self-renewal were on the whole more impressive than those of many younger composers.

THE REVOLUTION CONTINUES

Hans Werner Henze (born 1926) remained true to the left-wing political stance of his life and music. His opera *The English Cat* (1983) was a satire on capitalist and middle-class society in Victorian England, with the characters portrayed as cats. Henze's Ninth Symphony (1997), using voices with an orchestra like Beethoven's Ninth, was a fierce condemnation of Germany's Nazi past.

Henze at the 1982 Aldeburgh Festival

A STRING QUARTET WITH A DIFFERENCE

The passage of time did not reduce the avant-garde notoriety of Germany's Karlheinz Stockhausen (born 1928). In 1977, he had started work on *Licht* (Light), a vast cycle of seven operas, one named after each day of the week. This is now almost complete, with only *Sonntag aus Licht* (Sunday, from Light) remaining to be written. One of the scenes of *Mittwoch aus Licht* (Wednesday, from Light, 1992–98) was the already legendary *Helicopter String Quartet* (1993), where the four members of a string quartet each play their music in one of four helicopters linked with each other by closed-circuit television.

WIDER ACCEPTANCE
Stockhausen's music has at last begun to make headway in established circles. A major retrospective of his work was mounted at the 1995 Salzburg Easter Festival.

QUIET SOUNDS

In the mid-1970s, Italy's Luigi Nono (1924–90) had abandoned the left-wing political content of his earlier music. He now wrote several very sparely composed works which seemed to be searching out the quietest essence of musical sound itself. The largest of these was the semi-theatrical *Prometeo* (Prometheus, 1984). Others included *Fragmente-Stille – an Diotima* (Fragments-Silence – to Diotima, 1980, dedicated to Nono's daughter), and *No hay caminos, hay que caminar...* (There are no pathways, only the travelling itself..., 1987) for seven instrumental groups.

THE REVOLUTION PAUSES

Nono's apparent rejection of his own previously firm political views made some people think his career was past its best. Others admired his readiness to explore different musical territory.

NEW MASTERWORK

Berio's latest opera or azione musicale (musical happening), Cronaca del Luogo (Chronicle of the Place) was premièred at the 1999 Salzburg Summer Festival.

BERIO AND OPERA

Luciano Berio (born 1925) continued to produce works showing his mastery of vocal and instrumental sound, over large-scale time-spans. He collaborated with the novelist Italo Calvino on two operas, *La Vera Storia* (The True Story, 1982) and *Un Re in Ascolto* (A King Listens, 1984).

ENGLAND AND SCOTLAND

The strongest English music continued to be created by maverick individuals whose work had little in common with that of their continental European colleagues. Scotland, too, now produced two prominent composers.

TIPPETT, BENJAMIN AND TURNAGE

Among the late works of Michael Tippett (1905–98) were the non-religious oratorio *The Mask of Time* (1982) and his fifth opera, *New Year* (1991). And there were two gifted newcomers. George Benjamin (born 1960), a pupil of Messiaen (p. 10), caused a stir with *Ringed by the Flat Horizon* (1980) for orchestra. His *Antara* (1987) is scored for chamber group and the recorded and computer-enhanced sound of panpipes. Mark-Anthony Turnage (born 1960) attracted international attention with two operas, *Greek* (1988) and *The Silver Tassie* (2000).

JAZZ-CLASSICAL FUSION
Turnage's music has roots in both the mood and techniques of jazz. Your Rockaby (1994) is a concerto for soprano saxophone and orchestra.

VIRTUOSO TALENT
George Benjamin is an expert pianist and conductor of his own and others' music.

UNDIMMED ENERGY
Tippett's late works included a Triple Concerto (1980) for violin, viola, cello and orchestra, and a Fifth String Quartet (1991).

ORTHODOX RELIGION, UNORTHODOX MUSIC

John Tavener (born 1944) composed music based on the ancient Byzantine chants of the eastern Orthodox church. His work for cello and strings, *The Protecting Veil* (1989), achieved a wide success. Tavener's largest musical statements included the monumental *Apocalypse* (1995) and *Fall and Resurrection* (1999), both for soloists, chorus and orchestra.

TWO SCOTTISH COMPOSERS

A Night at the Chinese Opera (1987) was the outstandingly inventive first opera of Scotland's Judith Weir (born 1954). Two others followed: *The Vanishing Bridegroom* (1990), based on a Scottish folk tale, and *Blond Eckbert* (1994), adapted from a 19th-century German novella (short story). In 2000, Weir completed *women.life.song*, a large-scale orchestral song-cycle for the soprano Jessye Norman. James MacMillan (born 1959) made his name with two impressive works, *The Confession of Isobel Gowdie* (1990) for orchestra, and *Veni, Veni, Emmanuel* (1993) for solo percussionist and orchestra.

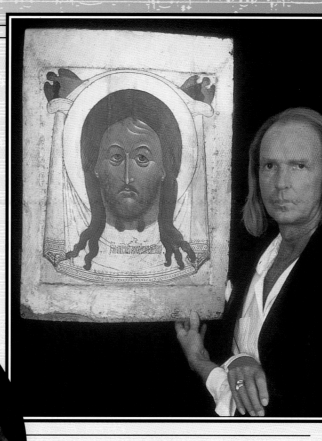

IMAGES OF THE DIVINE
For Tavener, a Byzantine Church icon symbolizes what he tries to achieve in his music: the total absence of a composer's personal pride, and instead a direct connection with ultimate religious truth.

A TRUE THEATRE COMPOSER
A scene from English National Opera's 1994 staging of Judith Weir's Blond Eckbert, *which explored dark themes of separation and mistaken identity.*

MEMORIAL

The funeral service of Diana, Princess of Wales in 1997 launched two pieces of music into superstardom. Elton John performed a specially adapted version of his song 'Candle in the Wind'. Within a few weeks it had sold 33 million copies and topped the charts in 22 countries. And John Tavener's choral *Song for Athene* (1993), too, made its composer internationally famous.

Princess Diana (centre) with the London City Ballet. She was their loyal patron.

EASTERN EUROPE: COMMUNISM AND AFTER

The collapse of Communist power in eastern Europe meant that at last, there was freedom to compose without risking official disapproval. But there was also widespread economic and social chaos, besides bleak memories of the past. Music often reflected this.

ESTONIAN ORIGINAL

Pärt has said: 'I could compare my music to white light which contains all colours. Only a prism can divide the colours...this prism could be the spirit of the listener.'

VOICE OF HIS PEOPLE

Giya Kancheli's large musical output includes six symphonies. He has described his task as a composer as 'filling spaces that have been deserted'.

A VOICE FROM ESTONIA

By the early 1980s, Estonia's Arvo Pärt (born 1935) had developed a personal style derived partly from eastern Orthodox chant (like John Tavener's music, p. 27). Pärt's *Cantus in memoriam Benjamin Britten* (1980), for strings and a single, tolling bell, was followed by other successes, including his *St John Passion* (1982) for soloists, choir and instruments, and the liturgical *Kanon Pokajanen* (1997) for unaccompanied choir. His music often appears on the ECM record label (p. 22), which is a major force in modern music.

KANCHELI AND SCHNITTKE: A TRAGIC HERITAGE

Giya Kancheli (born 1935), from the Republic of Georgia on Russia's southern border, is another composer much recorded on ECM. His style is rooted in Georgian folk music, whose lyrical sadness is often presented within a bleak and spacious orchestral landscape, as in *Mourned by the Wind* (1989) for viola and orchestra and *Abii ne viderem* (I turned away so as not to see, 1994) for viola and strings. Russia's Alfred Schnittke (1934–98) drew together extremes of different musical styles in response to the repressive absurdity of Communist society around him. Major examples are his Fourth and Eighth Symphonies (1984 and 1994).

LYRICAL GIFT
Elena Firsova (born 1950) is probably the most gifted Russian composer since Dmitri Shostakovich (1906–75), with a quieter and more lyrical style than that of many of her contemporaries. Two of her finest works set words by the Russian poet Osip Mandelstam: *Earthly Life* (1986) and *Before the Thunderstorm* (1994).

Elena Firsova now lives and works in England.

TORTURED SOUL
Schnittke's response to the hostile political world around him was to compose ceaselessly. He produced nine symphonies, fourteen concertos of various kinds, and four operas including Life with an Idiot *(1992) and* Gesualdo *(1995).*

SCHNITTKE'S DREYFUS – J'ACCUSE
Dreyfus was a 19th-century French officer who was unjustly convicted for treason. Schnittke's 1994 opera also refers to J'accuse, *the pamphlet in Dreyfus's defence by the writer Emile Zola.*

KURTAG: COMPRESSED STRENGTH

The music of Hungary's György Kurtág (born 1926) is highly concentrated, while also able to build impressively large structures with only small vocal and instrumental forces. *Messages of the Late Miss R. V. Troussova* (1980) is a major song-cycle for soprano and ensemble. Kurtág's *Kafka Fragments* (1986) is an hour-long work for just a soprano voice and a solo violinist.

GLOSSARY

AVANT-GARDE An artistic style more challenging than the conventional ones of the time.

CANTATA An Italian term for a work using voices – literally, 'something sung'.

CHAMBER MUSIC Music played by a group of solo players.

FLUGELHORN (from the German word for a 'winged horn'). A brass instrument with the full, rounded sound of a bugle, but with the keyed mechanism of the trumpet.

FRESCO A technique of painting on a plaster wall, often in a church. It often presents a narrative story-line in visual terms, from left to right.

FUSION A term used in jazz and rock to describe the 'crossover' of different musical styles.

LEFT-WING Used to describe socialist or communist political views. 'Right-wing' describes conservative political views.

LITURGICAL A piece of choral music based on a text from a religious service.

MODERNISM Music that sounds modern compared to what had come before.

OCTAVE The musical interval (or range) covering the twelve notes of the western scale. The modern piano has a range of just over seven octaves.

ORATORIO A large-scale setting of a text, usually on a religious subject, for solo voices, chorus and orchestra.

PANPIPES An instrument consisting of tubes of different length, played by blowing across the tops of the open ends. Named after the Ancient Greek god Pan, they are a popular folk instrument, particularly in the Andes mountains of South America.

SONG-CYCLE A collection of songs designed to be heard together as a single work. Some song-cycles have a narrative story-line.

STRING QUARTET A work for four instruments; also the group that plays them. A string quartet consists of two violins, viola and cello.

SYMPHONY Traditionally, an orchestral work in four movements, but it can be expanded to include extra movements and solo and choral voices. There are also one-movement symphonies.

TIMELINE

	MUSICAL EVENTS	THE ARTS	FAMOUS MUSICIANS	MUSICAL WORKS
0	•First Castle Donington rock festival, UK	•Millions see J.R. Ewing shot in Dallas TV series	•Deaths of John Lennon and Bon Scott (AC/DC)	•John Adams's Harmonium
1	•The Rolling Stones' Tattoo You tour of US	•Steven Spielberg's film Raiders of the Lost Ark	•Death of songwriter Hoagy Carmichael	•The Police's album Ghost in the Machine
2	•Michael Jackson's Thriller tops the charts	•Alice Walker's novel The Color Purple	•Robert Plant releases his first solo album	•McCartney's and Wonder's song 'Ebony and Ivory'
3	•The Police worldwide Synchronicity tour	•Barbra Streisand stars in the film Yentl	•Thin Lizzy splits up	•Steve Reich's The Desert Music
4	•Première of Tippett's The Mask of Time	•David Lean's film A Passage to India	•Deaths of Marvin Gaye and Count Basie	•Bruce Springsteen's Born in the USA
5	•Live Aid concert in UK and Philadelphia	•Death of Marc Chagall, Russian-French painter	•Singer Ricky Nelson killed in a plane crash	•Sting's Dream of the Blue Turtles
6	•Exiled pianist Horowitz plays in USSR	•Claude Berri's film Jean de Florette	•Death of Thin Lizzy singer Phil Lynott	•Messiaen's Livre du Saint Sacrement
7	•Madonna tours UK for the first time	•Tom Wolfe's novel The Bonfire of the Vanities		•George Michael's album Faith
8	•Nelson Mandela 70th birthday party concert	•Barry Levinson's film Rain Man	•Madonna stars in Speed the Plow on Broadway	•Van Halen's album OU812 •Turnage's opera Greek
9	•The Who go on tour after a seven year gap	•Amy Tan's novel The Joy Luck Club	•The Rolling Stones re-group after four years	•Madonna's album Like A Prayer
0	•First 'Three Tenors' concert, in Rome	•Kevin Costner's film Dances with Wolves	•Deaths of Luigi Nono and Leonard Bernstein	•Prince's album Graffitti Bridge
1	•Bryan Adams spends 15 weeks at UK No. 1	•National Gallery opens Sainsbury wing in London	•Prince forms the New Power Generation	•Stephen Sondheim's Into the Woods
2	•Freddie Mercury 'AIDS Awareness concert'	•St Lucian writer Derek Walcott wins Nobel Prize	•Death of Olivier Messiaen	•Messiaen's Eclairs sur l'au-delà
3	•Lloyd Webber's Sunset Boulevard opens	•Steven Spielberg's film Schindler's List	•Gallagher brothers form Oasis	•Andrew Lloyd Webber's Sunset Boulevard
4	•Second 'Three Tenors' concert, in Los Angeles	•Death of film-maker Jean-Louis Barrault	•Death of Nirvana's Kurt Cobain	•Judith Weir's opera Blond Eckbert
5	•John Tavener's Apocalypse premièred	•Irish poet Seamus Heaney wins Nobel Prize		•Jethro Tull's album Roots to Branches
6	•The Sex Pistols reform for Filthy Lucre tour	•Death of British artist Helen Chadwick	•Buena Vista Social Club record their first album	•Elliott Carter's Symphonia for orchestra
7		•First of J.K. Rowling's Harry Potter books		•Hans Werner Henze's Ninth Symphony
8	•Buena Vista Social Club perform in US	•Birthday Letters by English poet Ted Hughes	•Deaths of Michael Tippett and Alfred Schnittke	•Stockhausen's opera Mittwoch aus Licht
9	•Berio's opera Cronaca del Luogo premièred	•Building of London's Millennium Dome		•Will Smith's album Willennium

INDEX